PIANO & HERRINGS
BILL ELLIOTT

Published by The People's Press of Milton Keynes.
Care of 53 Cambridge Street, Wolverton, Milton Keynes
MK12 5AE.

ISBN O 904847 00 4

Acknowledgements

Bill Elliott's autobiography was compiled from more than seven hours of tape-recording, collected and transcribed by Roger Kitchen with some assistance from Ivor Goodson.

The People's Press wish to thank Angela Easter and Jennie Harwood for typing and retyping drafts of the manuscript, Robert Ayers and the Wolverton and District Archaeological Society for their help and permission to reproduce photographs from their collections, and Milton Keynes Development Corporation, especially Messrs. John Platt and Peter Waterman for their support and generous financial assistance to this project project.

Chapter 1
CHILDHOOD

My name is Arthur William Elliott. I was born at Great Linford on July 27th, 1884. There were 4 brothers besides me. My father's father was a smith's striker in the Works. He used to love his beer. I remember my grandmother told me that he used to go to the Nag's Head Pub at Linford and come home drunk and she used to get hold of his trousers and shake the money out and pull the mat back over the top of it. When he got up in the morning he knew how much money he'd got.

My grandmother used to be postmistress in Linford. I slept there once or twice in that house and when she packed up after her husband died she went and got an alms house and I went over and stayed with her at times. I remember it was only one room, a four poster bed and curtains pulled round, a leather sofa under the window. There was a spring down below where we used to get the drinking water, a good spring it was. My father had to go down to that spring from half way up Linford High Street. They got me a kitten and they caught me dipping its head in one bucket and then in another.

My mother's father lived in London. He'd got a contractor business in horses and carts and they sold up. His daughter, my Aunt Annie, married a farmer who lived near Rugby and he moved there and carted all his furniture by his own horses and carts. We used to go as youngsters when we had August Holiday, we had 7 days then, I used to love it. We used to go to the farm to pick the eggs up, it was lovely.

My father used to go crow starving up at Linford Wood when he was 7 years of age.

Years ago when the farmers had sown the corn in the fields there were a lot of crows and they used to have these boys up the fields to keep yawking and shouting at them, walking across the field to frighten them off; of course the crows used to pick the grain up from the ground. What they have now is a gun firing off every so often. In that period we used to have a winter and summer, we don't get it now.

My grandmother, I heard her say, used to have to cook my dad a roly-poly, jam one end and meat the other end. He used to go to the house, if they were working near the farm, and ask for a basin of greens' water, and they'd put a bit of pepper and salt in it and they'd have that. It was that cold I've heard my father say he used to put this roly-poly under his arms with his hands in his pockets, and bite it.

My mother took a parlour maid's job at the Linford Rectory and that's how my father and she came to be picked up. She never said anything about her job there.

My father went into Wolverton Works as an apprentice coach fitter, brake fitter. At that period they used to build the engines and all. When Crewe opened my father had to go down there, when he was a boy of 16, and I heard him say, "My Sunday suit was a pair of corduroy trousers, a jacket and a waistcoat".

That's all he'd got for Sunday.

He got lodgings and he got on and he got into boxing, he had lessons in it and then he played rugby. He used to play rugby for Crewe Alex. I've been cricketing there at Crewe Alex in the cricketing competition of the Railway Staff. He said to me a long while after he'd finished work. "I'd like to go to Crewe Will".

I said, "I'll take you to Crewe".

So we got one of the chaps, Tom Jacks, to fix us up for the weekend. We went on the Friday night, the train used to take us free to Manchester. Dad met an old lady there, and was talking to her and saying this and that, and she was saying "Oh he's dead and So and So's dead and so and so's dead and he's left here".

So any road, the Saturday morning we had a walk round and we went round to the Railway Veterans like they've got here and he started making enquiries there. Not a soul did he know but they were all dead. He was near 80 then when I went down with him and mother. He never had a smell of anybody.

I was 4 years of age when we moved from Linford, we'd got another boy, and grandfather used to come and visit us on a Friday dinner time. He had an apple tree in his back garden, with those nice little red apples, early ones, and he used to bring them up in his pocket. Once he said to me, "Look here, you come over and see me, come over by yourself and bring your brother with you".

My brother was only a little dot, and grandfather said, "I'll give you 6d each".

And the time came when we went over. By the Redbridge Field, opposite to the road, on the left side going to Newport there were some elm trees, it was a holiday and there'd been some Germans come round with a bear, Catchipoli. This bear and the bloke were lying under these trees, we saw the bear and we ran like hell, we were only kids!

When we came from Linford to Wolverton we lived at 507 Young Street and mother made friends with the people who lived at the end house as you go down to the Goods Shed, name of Rathbone. I remember father coming home one Friday and telling mother he was going to America and I remember her crying like the devil and she went down to this Mrs. Rathbone to get consolation!

He went to America with the two coaches out of here to the Chicago Exhibition. He went in 1893 and he was out there from the January and he came back in the December and I remember him telling me that they'd got skyscrapers then, like they've got here now.

He said, "The fires they used to have!".

He'd seen dozens and dozens of people clasped together and jumping off a 16 or 17 storey building and kill themselves rather than be burned. He went under the Niagara Falls and had a good trip round.

I remember when he came home it was just before Christmas and mother had made friends next door but one, name of Mrs. Abbot, Joe Abbot was her husband's name and she made some little pigs out of pastry, and I told Dad when he came home, "We've got some pigs in the sty".

Before he left he had started negotiations on the ground of the house at 28 Cambridge Street and mother had it all to do after he'd gone. When the house was completed we had Sam Holland's Sentinel Steam Engine to draw our furniture up in that house. There was only one living in that street, and that was in a house straight opposite us, 27, his name was Craig. The house was built by a Leighton Buzzard firm.

I remember going in there one day when the builder was putting the floors down and he'd got two cramps and he was cramping them all up together, all tongue and grooved. They were good houses, there were 6 or 8 of them. There was us, Abbot, Stiles, Dixon . . . . . . When I sold that house those

3

boards were still all close together. They used to put the wood on the site and all diagonally crossed to dry out but nowadays it's all wet, the blinking boards are all apart and they're not tongued and grooved, they're all just done square. Those houses were built.

I sold that house for £1220 and its been sold 3 times since then and fetched over £4000 the second time. It was all gas, it had never been converted to electric. Dad had a bathroom put in one of the bedrooms — there were 4 rooms upstairs.

Mum had to work hard with 5 boys. The other work used to fall on me. I always had to turn the mangle, clean the grate and polish it and go on all the blinking errands. When the youngest one came he'd just started to stand up by the chair. I was, as usual, turning the mangle and I remember him running out to his mother in the scullery. I remember her picking him up, "Oh, you little duck", she said.

That was his first run on his own.

I used to go round with milk at Bradwell and I used to sell the 'Birmingham Daily Argus' at night round the houses at Wolverton. I was about 12 then. We used to have a coal range and I had to get up, clean the ashes out, especially on Saturdays and Sundays. I used to be the one who used to get all the errands. There's one price I remember. I used to have to get 6 pound of moist sugar in a blue paper bag for 10½d.

Dad didn't do many jobs around the house. He used to run the allotment. Before these houses were built there used to be railings right from the Stratford Road to the end of Buckingham Street right up to Green Lane. That used to be allotments then.

Dad used to keep bees there and I was there with him one day and one bee crawled up my blinking knickers and stung my leg. I was wiping my nose up there once and a bee stung me right on the nose . . . . oooh!

My old dad, he used to have a side of bacon and ever so many hams hanging up in the kitchen. We used to live then! Roly-polys — spotted dick we used to call them. It was all good food. I've had good food all my life. That's what kept me going, I expect. And I have good food now — as far as I can get!

I remember getting a hiding one day. I'd been cricketing at Old Bradwell and we were carrying the gear back and there was a band contest in the Park (when the express went by you couldn't hear the blinking band). On the night we went down there they had a bit of a do and I was on this aerial runway and

we all had a go and of course I was the last to go and off I went
and I broke both my wrists, then I got a damn good hiding! Old
Dr. Miles down at Bradwell, he set them and I couldn't go to
the school prizegiving. I went to the bottom of the garden
waiting for it, standing on a step and looking over the wall.
They used to have splints then, and after your arm had been in
it so many weeks, you could pull the splint right off. I used to
pull it off and peel all the skin off.

Miss Gee taught me down in the school when it was in the
Market Hall and she's still alive today — 101 she is now. She
taught my kiddies as well. When my first one came in from
school she said, "Miss Gee's my teacher".

I said, "You tell Miss Gee when you go back, 'You used to
teach my daddy' ".

When she came back I said, "What did Miss Gee say to you?"
"She said, 'No I don't think so' ".

The teachers were alright, of course you could get a slap on
the ear'ole. They they used to have a cane. When you got the
cane you used to put a hair on your hand. We used to think
that would split the cane.

I wasn't very brilliant, I was more for sport.

I remember sitting out in the playground — I think we were
having model drawing. At the time they were rook shooting
and I was looking up at these. When they're shooting rooks the
rooks stand on the edge of the nest and they shoot them from
the nest. I was looking at these and the schoolmaster was talking
to me and of course I didn't know it. He came up to me and
said, 'Elliott you go in school and wait till I come'.

So when I got in school he got the cane out and gave 3 cuts
on each hand and hit the wrist on each hand. I'd just got over
breaking my wrists and I remember my mother going to him
the next day — didn't she chalk him off!

I remember one schoolteacher, his name was Fatty Davis.
He was a Welshman and I couldn't understand him properly
and I used to make a lot of mistakes.

There were 30 or 40 in the same class with 7 standards in the
school. But I never got there, I failed the 5th standard I think,
I had to stand down one year. Each year you moved rows.

They closed the school down there while I was at it and I
remember marching up to the new school in Church Street with
the other boys. They built another school because our other
school was too crowded.

Going to school of a Monday morning I used to write my

name on the desk in the dust. They only had one cleaner who used to sweep with a brush. It isn't like it today!

We started at 9 had a ¼ hour break at 10, then from 10.15 till 12. We had 2 hours break for lunch and then went from 2 till 4.

A chap named Harry York used to be a teacher. He was a devil, he was, he'd got a short cane, I used to have to run about for him, I used to take love letters to his girl who used to live at the end house just opposite the school.

Harry Lomax, he was a damn good teacher he was, you could tell at that age, you could tell when you'd got a good teacher and when you hadn't. You didn't know his qualifications or anything, but he used to be nice. Some of them used to be a bit hard, you know, they'd come round and give you a smack with the cane.

When you used to write, if your knuckles stood up, a teacher would come round and hit your knuckles.

Harry Hipsley was the headmaster. He was the choirmaster at the school. We used to have prayers in the morning and singing and occassionally the vicar used to come in and give a lecture. I didn't think much about that, talking about the Bible and so forth, I have never thought much about it — I think less of it today!

You never see any boys with patches now, I had patches on my knee, on my elbows, and everywhere else, and I remember my mother saying to me once. "Will", she says, "your clothes will never wear out while I keep patching them".

Everybody had patches on, they couldn't afford to buy clothes at that time.

We used to have trousers, short ones, and a jacket, a waistcoat and flannelette shirts. It was only the toffs who wore wing collars when you were dressed up on Sundays, like the Church and Chapel people, they used to come out dressed in top hats. Anybody who used to have a little job inside the Works used to have a top hat and a Bible under their arm and first thing they did when they got in the shop on Monday morning was to swear like a trooper!

"You made me swear I shall have to go next Sunday and get my sins forgiven".

There was no entertainment provided, we had to go to Sunday School and that was about it. That was just ordinary, singing hymns and somebody spouting about the Lord Jesus Christ and that, which I don't believe. Course, it's all a lot of tommy-rot —, it is honestly. How could anybody make heaven and earth? How could they take a bone out of Adam's ribs and make a woman? How could they feed a multitude of people on 3 loaves and fishes, and if Adam was supposed to be a white man, where did all the black men come from? How did they stop the River Jordan flowing?

Four of us went round all the churches in the district on Sunday mornings, we even went in the Catholic Church at Wolverton. It was just for a walk and a sit down and get back home for dinner. Everyone had to go to Sunday School then, all the children had to go, but they don't go now. We used to have classes in different ages and you had one teacher there and he used to read the Bible and we used to sing hymns and so forth. We used to sit up in the gallery when we got older and sing like blooming birds.

My mother wouldn't let me go in the choir at church. When I was at school the headmaster used to take us in singing lessons. We used to sing in four different tones, like a choir, and he used to stand behind me and listen.

To cut a long story short, one day he wrote a letter and asked me to give it to my mother. I took it home to mother and he asked permission for me to go in the choir and she said, "No".

I'd had half my tonsils out down at the doctor's, down old Doctor Miles', and in the finish I had to go into a London hospital to have the whole of my tonsils and adenoids out.

She said that my throat wouldn't stand it, but I always went yawking about in the back ways.

Two of us had catapults and we put a tin on the gate where we used to play football in that big field against the river bridge at Haversham. I got this here tin and we were catapulting it and Inspector Anthony and a Constable came along in a trap and stopped. They didn't get out.

"Give me them catapults and don't use them again".

They took them away from us and that's the only time as I've had anything to do with the law.

The weather is not like it used to be. My father, I remember him telling me while we lived down the Little Streets, he got on the River at Haversham bridge and skated right the way through to Buckingham. When I was a kid in Cambridge Street we used to have a slide down Radcliffe Street where the Square is. We used to start just against the Congregational Church, have a run down, and you could slide right down to what was Leason's shop — a good wide slide.

Chapter 2
WORK

When I first left school I started in the Works at 14, that was in 1898. I got 5/-d less 3d, that was as an office boy. They had boys for running about, they all had to do different jobs, some would go on a screwing gang, or in the smith's with a hammer, all that sort of business. You didn't go straight on to be an apprentice but they used to have apprentices come in from charities from Stony Stratford. They had to pay to come in to be an apprentice but we didn't. Anybody whose father worked there — and some of them had 7 or 8 kiddies — they could all go in as privileged apprentices after they had been through a 12-month period running about or doing these other jobs. Some of these jobs lasted 18 months, it all depended what they were on.

You chose yourself what trade you wanted to go into. I chose to work in the Finishing Shop because I liked woodwork. I used to do a lot of carving at one time. We had 2 regular carvers in our shop, they used to do a lot of carving for the Royal Train, Freddy Dunton and Bob Holland.

When I first started work it was from 6 o'clock in the morning till half past five at night. We used to work 6 till quarter past 8, then a break till 9 for breakfast, 1 till 2 for lunch and then on to half past five, 54 hours a week. They put you on a scale according to age and when you became 21, then you got the basic man's rate of 26/-d a week. It's different altogether now, it's like everything else, it's mass production now. There wasn't anything like that then. You had to work it all up by hand.

We used to make our own sliding doors for the railway coaches, they were a big job, they were all made of teak. We had to put the pillars in and clean the mortices out and then fit them in and knock them together. They were usually 6—8 sliding doors and perhaps a couple of toilet doors and the two end doors in each coach.

Each gang had their own job to do. We used to bore holes to put the net poles up for the nets for luggage — we'd wedge them and glue them up. That was all done by hand, but afterwards it was all done by presses. The work got easier, but we still had to carry the doors around.

In later years we changed to mass production. At first in 1924 or 25 it was a semi-mass production at first, and I was Chairman of the Shop Committee and spent a whole week pricing jobs. The Company paid my wages. I agreed with the foreman and with the management all the men's rates in the Works. There was only 4 or 5 that we couldn't agree on. The prices were to be p.p. (provisionally priced). So we did a good job of work. There was a lot of farthings, 1¼d jobs.

"Let's start", I said to the foreman, "by cutting them out".

I did the job on my own, I used to go round the gangs alone.

The only time we had Work Study was when we were making Assault Boats in the 2nd World War period. I was Chairman then of the Works Committee and it got so they couldn't agree with the prices in the Body Makers' Shop. To cut a long story short it got so that we had all the union bosses down and that was the only time we allowed time and motion. It was put down then that it was the first and the last time they allowed time and motion study, but they have it now. From what I understand the men who are doing the pricing now know nothing at all about the job — not a bit. There's been a hell of a lot of squabbles and they've had a strike or two.

Going to classes during work time has come through Trade Union business. The boys now have a day a week at school and the Railways have got their own apprenticeship scheme now. Outsiders come up here now, there was nothing of that with us. We had to learn the trade from the blokes we were working with.

As a boy I had a half-rip saw and it wanted sharpening and I took it into the Works. I knew that a chap named Williamson was a good saw sharpener and I took it in and I said, "Fred, would you set and sharpen this for me?"

"No", he says, "you can do it yourself".

So he showed me how to do it and I carried on, so I could sharpen a saw.

I was a devil for practical jokes. I used to buy sneezing powder from Northampton and stink bombs. I used to bang one of them about the shop. If you had a boy with you, you could send him to the Glue Wash for a bucket of cold steam.

There were a hundred apprentices sacked out of the Works one week and another 250 some weeks afterwards. I was in the 250. That was when the Railway Companies were doing badly. It isn't like it is today, the managers will keep the men even if they haven't got the work.

When I got the sack I got the Football Secretary and the Cricket Secretary to write down to Eastleigh because they were busy down there in the Railway Shop. They didn't want me, but I got back and had a letter from the Works to start back at work. There was a lot of people who went away and came back. They came back as soon as it got busy.

After the 1st World War had been on a bit they used to have brake vans and parcel vans and they used to knock the guts out of them, and we used to have to fit them up as hospitals, put the beds up and so on.

We had to work all night sometimes and you'd get home and get to bed and they'd come and fetch you out and you only had 2 or 3 hours sleep. We had worked the night before and then we worked the day and just got ready to go to bed and they came and fetched me out and our foreman was standing there and he says, "Come on Billy, there's a lot of wounded laying at so and so, get stuck into it".

You start as an ordinary boy or a man in the Union, then as you got older you attended the meetings and that's how I got involved. Trade Unions were not about much when I was an apprentice. I joined as a journeyman paying my dues each week. They collected in the Works, with a different collector in each shop. You attend a meeting after a bit of trouble in the shop and that's how I started.

When you get one job you get shoved into another job. I started in the Trade and Labour Council as a delegate. The NUR used to have a few members and of course there were always antagonistic to the Mechanics' Unions. We had about two or three delegates from each Union and we used to attend meetings at the Science and Arts Institute, once a month. That's how I started and it was through this that I was nominated for the Urban District Council. They nominated me for Calverton division. It had never been contested before and I got within 7 votes of winning. I had a lot of people come over with me and we gave them a good roust up on Saturday.

Then I tried again and got beat by 23 votes on that occasion.

It was a lovely day when we walked over there across the fields. We only went once to canvass, but of course a lot of people knew me over at Calverton because I worked with them.

The Executive of the Vehicle Builders' Union have a 3 year period then they have to go up for re-election. Any branch could nominate a member, so our branch nominated me. I had attended the Executive before, not as an executive member but out with the odds and sods. We had areas, there was Newport Pagnell, Peterborough, Lincoln, Nottingham, Derby, Northampton, Cambridge, Bedford, Luton and places like that formed the E. Midlands Division and they used to meet once a quarter. I used to go with our representative and that's of course how I got on, because they knew me. When I put up for the Executive they bunged me in. I didn't get in the first time, there was the Lord Mayor of Lincoln that I had to stand against, but he did something that he hadn't ought to have done in the Union, and of course, he got squashed, so that gave me an open chance, and with attending the meetings they knew me and I just got in as Executive member.

I had to attend these meetings and report the business of the Executive. I became President on 2 occasions — the President runs for one year, he can't be elected twice in succession.

I always used to take some of the vegetables up from my garden, and some flowers, I remember taking some of the gladioli bulbs that I bought from Holland to an Executive Meeting. I had to put them up on the luggage rack and put my case on top of them to keep the blinking things from hanging over me. I took them straight to the Head Office and saw the Caretaker there and asked him if he could put them around in the morning. The branch at Manchester had built an oval table and they put all the flowers inside it. When they walked in and sat down they said, "Cor blimey, Bill Elliott must be here".

I remember when we got married, on October 24th, we were full time and at Christmas time a notice was put up, "Ten Days' Holiday — Lock Out" — you had ten days' holiday and not a penny for it, no paid holidays. We were locked out because the Company was down on its takings, they used to make us pay for it.

In the 1930s I had very near a couple of hundred members unemployed round here and I used to have my papers come from the Labour Exchange. I had to take it all down, ledger it all and packet the money up for them. I had to go and fetch the money from the Co-op Bank if I hadn't got enough money in a safe I had here. People who'd signed at Wolverton came from Cosgrove, Deanshanger, Yardley Gobion, Potterspury, Beachampton, Calverton, Nash and all round here. They only came to sign once a week at the Exchange. To ease them I used to packet their money up on the Thursday night. The papers came from the Exchange on Thursday morning. I used to go to work and the wife used to pay them out in my office there. They broke the damn back gate down once. They were here at 7 o'clock in the morning waiting to come in at 9.

They got 10/-d a week from the Union and 18/-d a week from the State. The Union didn't have enough money to last through the Depression. They put ½d levy on all members per working day and 1d a working day later, then they had to put a £1.00 levy on. A lot of members ran out of the Union over that £1.00, it was astonishing. I lost nearly half of my membership over that.

Some of them who ran out would pass me in the street and look the other side. Some of them have never spoken to me since then! And there's one chap now, he's been finished some years and still he's got in his head, "You buggers cut my benefit down".

He was only 21 and he's finished work now so you can tell how long he's been holding it against me.

One chap gave me a smack in the jaw in the backway one day. He'd drawn his benefit and he came down to see me and he said, "I haven't had all me benefit" and I said, "Yes you have, here it is" and I showed him the ledger and it had, 'ten weeks at 10/-d and another ten weeks at a reduced benefit'.

I said, "There's your signatures", and he said, "They're not my signatures".

"Don't talk so . . . . ".

He'd got a girl in the family way and was out of work. I went down the garden with him and I said, "Look here mate you're getting trouble enough . . . . . . ".

And he did no more than give me a smack in the jaw and knocked me down. I was up and I ran him straight up the bloody back alley and he soon shot off.

We had a chap who was a Union Member in early 1925, and he got made a foreman down in the Machine Row. He was cutting the prices down on these machinists and they all carried on alarming about him. It got worked up and worked up and one thing and another, several things weren't right in the Works. He even went to one man in the urinal and told him

what job to do next. Then it came to the point when they got a
hammer and rang the buffers (the buffers are where they join
the coaches) and said "all out". Our shop committee had to go
down to the management and I explained to the Manager what
we'd come for. And he said "Well we're not going to shift that
foreman".

"Is that it?".

So we walked out into the Works. It was a stay-in strike, we
didn't go out. You could go out if you wanted to. They had
concerts and all that in the Works. The whole Works was out
for nearly a week.

The General Strike followed shortly afterwards. Those who
went in during the General Strike were called 'blacklegs'. There
was one bloke, we went on a trip on the yellow old peoples'
bus recently and we all trooped in for a cup of tea in a coffee
house and I said to the chap I was with, "Who's that bloke, I
know his face?".

"Oh", they said, "That's B.........., a painter".

"Oh" I says, "he came in during the bloody General Strike
didn't he?"

The Manor House Hospital at London, Golders Green, that
was a Trade Union business. It was about 2d a week we started
paying into the Hospital Fund. I knew some of the Officers
there so I went up and had a look round it once. I used to suffer
with the gout. My father left me that lot, he had it when he was
26 and he carried it right to his grave. It was a different hospital
altogether to going into a State hospital. It was run on
collections and membership. When I went in the nurse said,
"Come on then".

She took the particulars and she said to the doctor "Doctor
I've brought you a provincial member".

He said, "Oh bring him in, I'll be pleased to see him".

So he said, "What's your trouble, mister?"

I said, "Gout".

"Oh" he said, "We can cure that".

I said, "Do you think so? They can't cure Mr. Churchill".

They nearly killed me. They give me a quart bottle of
medicine and I had just taken another allotment over and I'd
been sweating up there, turning this up, cutting the gooseberry
bushes and plum trees down. I must have got a cold in my ribs
and I was having this medicine at the time and it upset my
kidneys.

In 1928, I remember it quite well, our branch made a

resolution asking for a 40 four week. We had reduced it a bit
from 54, in 3 or 4 different periods. It wasn't reduced much
the first time, then it was reduced — we started at half past 7
then we lost Saturdays. That was nearly all in my time. The
Railway Works was always behind the rest of the country from
this point of view. I remember meeting the employers, trying to
knock Saturday working off, and they told us, "If you knock
that off they'll go and work Saturdays for somebody else!"

This was proved true, there's a lot of people work Saturdays
and Sundays now on doing housework, building walls and
altering their houses.

We had three free passes a year and one 'foreign' pass. The
'foreign' pass was on other lines, the Great Eastern, Great
Western, Great Northern, Central and Southern — that pass was
for your holidays. They have more now, they can travel abroad
now free. I've only been abroad once. I took my daughter when
she was courting, over to France. I don't want to go abroad
again. My missus said, "Look, that woman's gone in the toilet
with a man!"

They can catch hold of a man's arm while he's piddling there!
I didn't like anything over there, you didn't know what money
you'd got.

As soon as we landed at Calais there were a lot of chaps with
silk scarves on the quay and my daughter went and bought one
of these and she gave him a 10 bob note or a pound note and she
came running back after she'd bought this "Look at the money
I've got Dad!"

I said, "It ain't worth much!"

I think the times are not far distant when the workers will
have a share in the management and it's right too. I agree with
that from every point of view. These time and motion men
know nothing about the job. When I was on the Works
Committee, if you'd got any suggestions to make or you wanted
to discuss anything relative to anything like that you could
always do it. I know when I made an application for smoking
in the Works, the superintendent sent for me and said, "What
do you mean by this? You know we had a blooming great fire
not long ago through cigarette smoking".

"How do you know it was cigarette smoking" I said.

Anyway we hammered it and hammered it until we got it,
then a lot of people said to me, "You was a bloody fool you
know Bill to get smoking, that's costing me a few bob a week!"

We used to have a fixed holiday in August, the first week in

August and I got that through in that you could have a holiday what time you liked. When it came for me to know what is was, there was one bloke out of my own Shop, he came to me and I said, "You can have it from the first week in May any time up to October"

He said "Right I'm a going to have the first week in May".

And he had a damn good week and all, and lovely weather.

Chapter 3
COURTSHIP & MARRIAGE

You got the opportunity to meet girls if you went to a 'three-penny hop'. We used to have a threepenny hop down at Bradwell at the Labour Hall where Hiorns the Builder was until recently. They used to have a piano and Arthur Watson used to play it and a little chap who used to work in the Time Office used to be M.C. We used to go there about 7 o'clock till 10 or 11 o'clock. If we had a long night it was alright because the next shop to that was an old lady who used to make coffee and cakes and we used to go trooping in there at half time. We used to dance ordinary Quadrilles, (they don't have it now) and the Waltz, Lancers and Waltz Cotillions.

When I was a boy at school we used to have to scrape a candle about 12 inches long, all off into a box. After 4 o'clock we'd take them across to the Science and Arts Institute, where they had a lovely large dance hall and sprinkle them all over the floor and then slide them in. That wasn't for our benefit; that was for the people's benefit for dancing — the school teachers used to do it.

It was at the threepenny hop that I picked up with my wife. She'd got a chap at the time. I was 21, she was 18. She started out to work in the refreshment room on the main LNWR at Crewe and she got the same amount of money as me when I started work — 5/-d a week, of course they provided her with overalls.

She could play the piano and she and her boyfriend came up to our house in Cambridge Street; that's where it started. In the end we said "Ta ta" to him. We had my 21st birthday then and we carried on from there.

We used to walk round the Old Road, but if you wanted a stile you had to be there early! But now it's altogether different, you don't see anybody out at night now. They wouldn't let me

and my girl stay in the front room, no fear, we had to come out!
I had a cousin come from Rugby, she was a bit younger than me,
we were in the front room and I heard old dad say, "Come
on out of there, come on out, you've no business in there!"
I could hear him telling Mother first, "What are they two
doing in there, go on fetch 'em out".
My wife and I were married at Bradwell.

*"Months after the wedding they found there were not legally
married . . . Miss Anne Trodd and Mr. Arthur William Elliott
turned up in good time for their wedding at St. James Church,
New Bradwell, but found that the church was completely
empty. After hurriedly arousing the Vicar, who had completely
forgotten about the wedding the couple were eventually
married, only to be told several months later that like 400 other
couples in the parish they were not legally married. That was 60
years ago and yesterday, Thursday Mr. & Mrs. Elliott of 49
Anson Road, Wolverton celebrated their diamond wedding
anniversary. They were married by the Rev. Newham Guest,
only the new vicar's second wedding at the Church in 1908.
It was several weddings later that Mr. Guest discovered the
marriage register being used at the Church was actually the one
for St. Peter's Church, Stanton Low. St. James' Church was not
licensed for the solemnization of marriages. An Act of
Parliament was hurriedly passed declaring all the marriages at
the church legal".*

That was what the "Wolverton Express" said about it.

There was nothing special about the engagement, I just
bought her a ring and that was that. I never said anything to her
mother or father. My chargehand got me the ring from somebody in London after I got the size of her finger. Her parents
knew we wanted to get married because I was making furniture
for our house.

When we were married we had our present house in Anson
Road to live in. I had it built when I was 22. I was 24 when I
got married, she was 21.

I've been married 67 years come October. My missus can't
take a joke, you can't pull her leg, but we've always been like
that. She goes for me sometimes and I go for her! I don't like
all this here sloppy-sloppy stuff, I never have done. I call a
spade a spade.

I saved £50.00 before I was married and borrowed £10.00
from my father to put down as a deposit on this house. You
hadn't enough money to save up before you were married to

get furniture. 99 out of 100, as long as they'd got a chair and a table and a bed and ordinary things, there were happy. Oh no, its not like today, they want a new house, fully furnished and a motor car, how they do it I don't know. I never used to spend anything. I didn't used to drink; I used to have perhaps half a pint or a pint and go and have a game of billiards in the Club if I didn't have anything else to do, but in the summer time I was always out. In the winter time I did boxing and I used to attend the Science and Arts Institute for wood carving and drawing.

The Wolverton Building Society was practically all done by employees of the Works. The man who was head of it was named named Fitzsimons and the Secretary was named Watson. I remember when I got my deeds I had to go up to the Works to see him and I wanted to borrow £200. I'd got £40 and my father lent me £10, so I had to put £50 down. Then, when everything was completed they sent for me up to the offices and Mr. Fitzsimons gave me the cheque and I had to take that to the bank. They gave me this here £200 in golden sovereigns and I remember them weighing it. I had to come and pay the builder, who lived where Winsor and Glave is now, his name was George Hebbs.

The third house from here, my pal, he bought that. We used to go cricketing together, footballing together and we used to go cycling together and we used to see how much money we could put in the bank monthly. Sometimes it was 5 bob sometimes 10 bob and sometimes a bit more.

My children, they carried on practically the same as I did. They had to make their own enjoyment outside, playing in the back ways. They had scooters — I made 3, and I'd got 4 of them, but the youngest one could only just walk. At that period I used to have to do their own shoe mending and after they'd had these scooters a few weeks, periodically I'd look at the shoes to see they were alright, and blimey, one foot was worn through!

I said to the missus, I said, "Look here, I'm not having that". As we had a copper in the kitchen there at that time, I smashed the scooters up and put them under there, so when they came down in the morning, they wanted to know where their scooters were and we said, "Somebody must have pinched them".

I remember them, they used to dress up with their mother's shoes and any old frocks she'd got out, and they used to have flower shows — 'a pin to see the flower show' — they'd have to give a pin to pay to come into the garden to see the flower show. They used to go bathing down at Haversham Viaduct. There used to be a saying, 'Bathe in May, buried in clay'.

The only education you could get was these schools, and from then it was like the miners or anybody else. Those who lived in the mining areas went down the mine, and the same with the girls in this area, they went to the Printing Works, the same with the boys in this area they went in the Railway Works, with a few women going into the Works in the polishing room and stitching room. It's what you might call your environment, you have to fall in with it, grow up with it.

My children were girls, a girl's different to a boy, a boy can get on, but I always say that those people who spend a lot of money on a girl, it's money thrown away. They get married and they're lost. Women never used to go into blinking factories, only the single girls but not married women, they always used to have to stop at home and look after the kids.

I can't see how this Womens Lib can really work. A man's home and can say "I'm finished for today", but how can a woman finish for today, who's going to rush up and take over? A man can't, not after a day's work, a woman can come and sit down in the garden all afternoon if she likes . . . you can't draw the line. It's the prerogative of nearly every married woman if she hasn't any children today to go to work. You've only got to walk down the street to see the milk bottles outside the house of a morning.

My daughters all went in the Printing Works. My wife's brother lived down at Bradwell this side of the Club on that same side. He was the Secretary of the National Deposit down there and his wife was a schoolteacher and they came up here several times and asked us if we'd let our eldest daughter go down there and live with them and I said "No I can't. I would, but I've just been and bought her a piano from London. She's having piano lessons, I'm not throwing that money away".

They hadn't got any children and in the end they persuaded me, there was a good home for her there and an outlook for her to get on. Any road she went down there and stopped there till she got married.

The second daughter stopped in the Printing Works until she was married. The other 2, they also went into the Printing Works. The youngest one came home one day, she was working in the envelope room, using the gum, and she pushed her

Mother with myself and
brothers Fred and Walter
in about 1891. A
photograph by Harry
Bartholomew.

School at the Market Hall, Wolverton 1897, with headmaster Harry Hipsley.
(I am fourth from left in second row).

Wolverton Town Football Club 1907-1908
'(I am seventh from left on second row).

The three Elliott brothers after a Whit monday and Tuesday Sports at Wolverton
Park, with our "haul'. From left to right
Myself and Walter (runners) and Fred (cyclist).

Our Wedding Day
Photograph taken in the back garden of my wife's parents house in New Bradwell.

Wolverton Science and Arts Institute, Church Street, now the site of a car park.

One of Sam Holland's engines similar to the 'Sentinel' which took our furniture from Young Street to Cambridge Street.

The Square in Wolverton, much changed in recent years.

nostrils together and they stuck with the gum. So I said, "I'm not going to have that, you can pack that job up, you can go into service, both of you".

Any road I fixed them up and got them a job with a Lord Somebody, he was a big man in accountancy. All my daughters were taught to cook, they could cook anything they were given, same as the wife. It cost me 40 quid to rig them up, they had a big trunk, two of everything — and 40 quid was a hell of a lot of money in those days.

When the second one was courting, her young man had a motorbike, and I remember him sitting on the bike here and talking to her. I went by them and took no notice of them. Any road, sometime afterwards her mother, my wife, fetched him in, and from that he stopped in!

He used to come here when he liked. He bought a car, a second-hand one, a Rover, and he took us down to see my two daughters who were down in Kent. We went in, there was one of my daughters, she'd got 8 ducks there on the table, we'd got there fairly early and when she saw us she started crying. She'd got to do these jobs ready for dinner at night. We stopped there for a bit and I think they made us stop for lunch. The Lady sent for us and we went upstairs and I remember they'd got some flowers on the table and they were 4 or 5 times the size of mine. She took us and showed us the park and I remember her saying, "that turf is over 400 years old". They had 9 gardeners there, they had big gardens and a big thatched place where they put their apples in and she showed me and the missus round.

My daughter used to go to London in the winter time, in their London house and then they both got so as they wanted to improve themselves and the eldest one left there and went to a Dr. Gilliat in Harley Street, as cook and we've still got some coffee here now what she gave us! Then she went from there to Lord Lukes at Pavenham, the Bovril magnate, she went there as a full cook. She took my wife and other daughter to Faversham for the interview with Lady Luke and was given the job and she stayed there until she married the second chauffeur from there. The youngest of them all went as parlour maid to Lord and Lady Fitzwilliam in Windsor Great Park.

Chapter 4
MY SPORTING LIFE

Many people have asked me my recipe for life, and many people come to me today. I tell them that it's good food, clean living and hard work. I've always worked all my life and when I was a young chap if it wasn't work it was football, cricket, running and all that. I was all the while on the go.

I would sooner live now because my life was sport. We never had any sport at school, all the sport we had was one football team. But now they play football and running and javelin throwing and the blinking lot — that would have suited me down to the ground. We never had a cricket team at school. When I was a boy Wolverton Town Cricket Club used to be down where Dr. Filde's house is now in Green Lane. They'had a carriage, a coach from out of the Works, set on trestles, and that used to be the pavilion for them. And at night when they were practising, I used to go down from Cambridge Street, running after the balls, fetching them up. And I know several of the men now as used to play, a man named Harry Lloyd, Alf Archer, schoolmaster Harry Hipsley, Dick Packer, I remember them quite well.

My sporting life started after I had left school. At about 16 my mother wouldn't let me play football because I had my tonsils out and the adenoids from my nose. I had half my tonsils cut out at Bradwell with old Dr. Miles. I sat there, he must have frozen it, I sat down and he did it and he took them out and put them on the table top. I went as white as a sheet.

So my mother wouldn't let me play football, but anyway after a bit I used to play, kicking a ball about and that, and then I started playing football. I bought my boots, stockings, shinguards and knicks and let somebody else keep them. I played ever so many games and we formed a club which we called the 'Albions' and we had headquarters at the North Western Hotel at the back where a man made organs. That used to be our dressing room and training room.

We had the playing field down against the river as you go to Haversham on the right hand side. We played Hanslope at Hanslope at the side of the 'Watts Arms' one Saturday afternoon.

My dad came home on Monday dinner time, and we were having our dinner, the 5 of us children sat round, the youngest one in the high chair. We were getting through our dinner and all at once dad says, "I was told that one of my boys was over at Hanslope last Saturday afternoon footballing and I'm goin' round the table to see who it was".

He saw the little one in the high chair and I remember him saying, "It's no use asking you if you were there".

And he said to the next one, (he lives in London now), "Was it you?"

He said, "No dad, I wasn't over at Hanslope".

He turned to the next one, he lives along Aylesbury Street, and he said "No dad, I wasn't at Hanslope".

He turned to the next one and he said "Was it you?"

"No I wasn't at Hanslope".

He turned to my next brother, Fred, and he said "Was it you then at Hanslope?"

He said, "No I wasn't at Hanslope".

He says "Oh well, it's only one left now, isn't it?"

He said, "Were you at Hanslope?"

I said "Yes dad"

"What were you playing then?"

"Football" I said.

"What were you playing in?"

"Football boots, shinguards and knicks".

He said "Where are they now then?"

I said, "So and so's got my boots, somebody's got my shinguards and somebody's got my knicks".

"Go and get them".

I thought he was going to put them on the fire. Anyway I went and got them and after then it was alright, I was allowed to play football.

In that period I know we had a good referee, he came from Leighton Buzzard. We were down there playing in the league and he came refereeing us and before half-time he comes up to me and says, "What are you doing playing down here, why aren't you playing for Wolverton?"

I said "Damn Wolverton, I don't want to play for Wolverton".
He said, "You will".
I said, "I shan't mate. No, I don't want any truck with
Wolverton Football Club".

Any road, next year, of course, I was with Wolverton! He
refereed a match down there and he came up to me and said,
"There you are, what did I tell you?"

I could play in any position, barring goal. We used to play in
Wolverton Park and they were in the North Bucks League and
the Ascot League and later in the Northants League. We did not
do very well in that league because most of them were pros.
When I finished playing with them I finished up with Bradwell,
and I think we won the Berks and Bucks Junior Cup while I was
playing with them. In one match with Wolverton we played, I
think I was outside right that day, Peterborough City were
down the Park, that was in the Northants League, they're pros
in there. That match with Peterborough City always stands out
in my mind. We beat them 12 − 2. Otherwise it was just the
ordinary run of things, one Saturday was like another Saturday.

I used to have a day out of work to do my 40 pole allotment
when I wanted it. When I used to play football for Bradwell I
said "I've got to get on with my garden, I shan't play on
Saturday".

Of course, there were plenty of unemployed at that time and
they said, "Oh we'll send a chap up there".

His name was Sickle Saunders and he came up and did all my
digging for me, so I could play football for them.

I very rarely used to get knocked down, and I didn't used to
slide, but my pants were always splashed, and the wife used to
always moan about it of course.

I could run in those days and there were two chaps in the
Wolverton team, Dick Westley and Tommy Dickens, they were
both runners at the time and they sadly wanted to take me on,
training me, but I wouldn't have it. I kept on with my boxing,
football and so on. There's nothing much more I can say about
football. When I played for Wolverton I just got an Ascot
League medal, otherwise it was just ordinary Saturday business,
although we won the North Bucks League several times.

In the summertime I played cricket. I started playing down
at Green Lane, where Dr. Harvey's house is built on, when I was
a boy still at school. Afterwards I started cricketing up in the
town, up at the top where the Town's field is now. I was 16, I
joined the Club and I played in the first match, 'Married versus

Single'. Afterwards I got on and started playing for the Second Team and then I got into the First Team. With the second team we were in the North Bucks League, which I think still runs, and we won that each year. Any road, I got promotion and was doing very well thank you. I won the batting average one year and the bowling average the next year. I was never lucky enough to get a century. I got 98 not out. We used to have day matches. I remember once playing Jesus College, Oxford because the Vicar here, Harnett, was taught there and got them to come and play us.

We used to go to Whittlebury, they had a professional there and they picked good men all round. We used to have a day match there: we had the lunch out in the pavilion with butlers there serving out from the house. I believe the House now has turned into a school. The Coopers used to keep that and they were sheep farmers and had got one son. They started cricket and they had the ground laid out and done with sand called 'Red Mole' which you can get all nice and level.

The deers used to run in that park, I don't know whether they do now or not. We used to have a good do there. We always looked forward to that. I remember we were there one Whitsuntide, Whit Saturday, and Mr. Cooper said to our Captain, Jonah Brown, "Have you got 2 men you could let us have for Whit Monday, we're playing the Puxley Hunt?"

He says, "Yes, I dare say we can find you a couple".

I don't know whether he'd been and asked anybody else but he came and asked me and I said, "Yes, I can come".

And then he asked another chap who used to be the school caretaker here, Freddy Rich and he said, "Yes".

My eldest daughter was in long clothes then, that would be about 1909.

Freddy had got a niece staying with him and they'd got a baby, so we decided that we'd see if we could get a wagonette, and we took the kids and the wives to Whittlebury. My wife was carrying our daughter and Lady Cooper came up to her and took the kid out of her arms and sent the butler in the house for an armchair and she sat down there. There were some bananas on the table and I thought, "I should like one of them".

But I didn't know how to damn well eat it, and with these butlers and footmen waiting on you I left it! There was plenty of whisky and anything you wanted but I didn't drink much then. Mr. Cooper won the toss and he came to me and said,

"Elliott, what position do you go in for Wolverton?"

I says, "First wicket down sir".

He says, "Alright, you can go in first for us".

I went through the innings, 30 not out, the others didn't get many!

He said, "You bowl don't you?"

"Yes" I said.

"Well you can start bowling then".

I had 5 wickets for 30 and we had to bat again and I got 45 not out the second innings, so I did pretty well with it.

There was a man living at Hanslope Park, name of Burr, he was a financier of some sort and they started up Dover coalfields and he went to live down there. He invited our club, Wolverton Town Club to go down and play his team. We went down there on the Friday and there was some King or Queen being buried that day, I remember that, while we were going through London. We arrived at Dover and were taken to a posh hotel and had dinner. We had a look around Dover then retired for the night, we left the hotel about 10.30 the next morning. We went to play them at Cricket, I think they beat us, we came back then to our hotel and Mr. Burr had arranged for the people from the theatre as they finished their turn to come into us and give their turn. It was Music Hall stuff and I remember they had a French woman there who was a yodler, I've never heard anything like it in my life! She yodled beautifully. We had some good artists and we had a good hotel. We went out sailing in the morning in the harbour and we got out so far and the damn wind dropped. We stopped there and one bloke said, "What about our breakfasts?"

I said, "Oh blow the breakfasts, we can get a breakfast tomorrow, but we can't get a sail tomorrow, we shall be home tomorrow".

We had a good do there all paid for.

We'd been playing cricket at Leighton Buzzard and we came back and there was a fair down at Bradwell. In those days there was always a boxing booth with them you know. I was there with two or three or more of the chaps and we stood watching them — and they wanted challengers to go in, so our kids collared me to go in. So, alright I went in and took my coat off and faced Snowball Somebody, from Kilburn I think it was, or somewhere in London! I could manage him alright, and after the second round somebody gave a cup to go round collecting for me, and dished it out after we finished three rounds. I got

4½d which was a lot of money in those days. I thought to myself "Well, I'll go down on Monday night and have another go at him".

So I went down on Monday night. Of course when they wanted to throw the gloves out I put my hand up and he shook his head, he wasn't going to have it! Now that was a professional!

Dad was a boxer, and I started in my younger years. Later on I bought a punch ball and set it up in our back garden. I used to go out after I'd had my dinner, punch this thing and there'd be some other training on at night, either football or cricket or running. There was a bloke came from Fenny Stratford up to my dad one dinner time and he said, "I've come from Fenny Stratford and I understand you've got two sons who are fairly good boxers. I'm running a competition, would you like to enter your sons in it?"

Dad said, "I don't know nothing about it or you, I don't know what sort of class you've got there".

He said, "I run a boxing class and I'm an ex-British Champion".

So dad said, "That's alright then. Can you fix up for us to come over and have a look at them?"

So they fixed up and we went over one Saturday afternoon.

He kept the 'Saracen's Head', that was the last pub going out of Fenny Stratford on the right hand side of the Watling Street. He took us the Saturday afternoon to the 'Bull and Butcher' that was another pub in Fenny. We went there and he'd got two from Woburn Sands, two from Bletchley and two from Fenny Stratford and he wanted us to match two of them. Dad said to me "You'd better have a go with the eldest one".

"Alright", I says so we get stripped out and started and he treated me like a blinking novice, saying, "Go on shoot 'em out, shoot 'em out".

I stopped and I said to my dad, "I can't get on like this".

So dad stepped in the ring and said, "Let 'im have it, go on get into him".

I started then and could deal with him then, the faster he went the better I was. My brother Fred didn't even put the gloves on. These other 6 or 7 that he'd got there to fight either of us, said "Uh, we're not going to fight them".

Any road he took us back to his pub and gave us tea and the one I fought couldn't eat his tea, saying, "I've hurt my jaw".

The ex-champion came up and saw my dad and wanted to let me go with him to the National Sporting Club in London and I was just turned 19 at that time. He came and asked me about it and at the time Pedlar Palmer — he was a lightweight British Champion — killed a man coming down the Bedford branch line from Newmarket Races, after a row, and that just put me off. If it hadn't been for that I'd have gone with him and I suppose I should have been dead myself by now if I'd gone.

Any road I could hold my own, didn't matter about who it was, bigger or not. I started here with a class up in the back bedroom of my house, I had a punch ball up there too. From there, that got too small for us, so I went over to Old Wolverton to a chap named Conway, who used to keep the Loco Pub there. He'd got some stables empty which the horses used to go in when they used to pull the boats along and I asked him if he'd let me have it for boxing of a night time. I bought 4 lamps and a gallon of paraffin and filled them up and hung them up on the walls for lights and started that off.

I used to walk over to Beachampton and give them instructions over there. I then went down the Park and took the Park dressing room. I used to go down there 2 nights a week in the winter time beside training for football. In the finish I got a place at the old tram depot halfway into Stratford. The trams stopped during the General Strike and never ran again. There was a chap in our shop he reckoned he could box and so we made up and we got the keys of that place. Anybody could come who liked and they could be taken on.

Saturday mornings 6 o'clock I'd walk over to Stony Stratford knock him up, he'd be ready, a bucket of water, a big sponge and we'd go down there. We used to have three rounds, sponge down, cold water, the steam used to rise up like it does off the horses when they've been racing, then walk home to breakfast. I've been boxing in Newport Pagnell, Olney, Buckingham, I used to get anybody as would come.

The following appeared in one of the local papers before the First World War.

ELLIOTT MEETS GODLEY IN A FRIENDLY ROUND

A sporting event of considerable interest was witnessed by a large number of members at the Stony Stratford Working-Men's Club on Friday evening. For some weeks strenuous endeavours have been made to revive interest on the sports side of the institution and particularly in the noble art. Under the guiding influence of Mr. A.E. FitzPatrick, himself a boxer of repute, and a pupil of Harry Webb, a winner of many contests, a number of enthusiasts have shown promise of becoming useful boxers.

One of the most promising of Mr. FitzPatrick's pupils is Godley, of Stony Stratford, a light-weight who possesses any amount of pluck, and he met A.J. Elliott of Wolverton, in a friendly bout on Friday. The Stony Stratford man was seconded by his trainer, Mr. FitzPatrick, and Elliott was assisted in this capacity by T. Beckett, of Wolverton. Mr. F. Joyce officiated as timekeeper.

The encounter took place in a large upper room of the club and extended over six rounds. Elliott was the "fancied one" of many, for besides having had more experience with the gloves he has a more powerful physique, and being inches taller than the Stony Stratford representative had a longer reach.

In the first two rounds the Wolverton man got in one or two vigorous punches which had their effect on Godley. The latter, however, attacked gallantly and even his alert opponent could not escape the blows directed at his head. In the third round Godley picked up wonderfully and gave almost as good as he received. The fourth round, however, was almost wholly in favour of Elliott. The fifth round was the best, for Godley showed up well. In the final tilt the Wolverton man gave of his best and repeatedly broke through the defence of Godley, whom whom he frequently drove into the corner. Elliott's was the most scientific display and he would have gained the victory as a cool resourceful boxer. Godley's was a game display, and with more experience he should develop into a useful man.

During the evening three-minute rounds were indulged in between Mr. FitzPatrick and H. Smith, Mr. FitzPatrick and Mr. Humphries, H. Smith and F. Kitchener, J. Coulton and C. Linden. The rest of the evening was spent in a convivial manner.

A CHALLENGE

Elliott's father, who lived at 28 Cambridge Street, Wolverton, and has three sons, challenges anyone in the district at boxing, cricket, bowling, cycling, running, football and billiards!

I was 27 when I took up running. On the cricket field I used to be out in the long field, if not bowling, because I could run. I hadn't got the time to do running doing all the other stuff, cricketing, boxing, the Institute, until I was about 23 or 24. When my brother started, he ran the ½ mile and mile, he gave me a pair of pumps, another brother gave me a jersey with

W.A.A.C. on it, and that's what started me running. I had 4
clocks in the room at one time that I'd won running. I won the
hundred yards and the 220 on the Whit Monday and I was
second in the 220 and third in the 100 on the Tuesday. I ran
for about 3 years. I ran at the Aston Villa ground and some
bloke shouted out "Good old Elliott" out of the crowd.

Young people aren't as happy as we were. In those days we
had to make our own enjoyment. On Shrove Tuesday we used
to go paper-chasing. A team would go off with bags on their
shoulders — in the first place they had to get the newspapers
and tear them up in little bits. Then we used to start off after
the hares, and they used to sprinkle a bit of paper as they ran
along. We, the hounds, had to follow where they'd dropped the
paper and you'd catch them before the finish if you could. We
used to go about 3 or 4 miles all across fields. We used to have
Shrove Tuesday afternoon from school, why I don't know.
Providing the weather was fine, and I could get on the ground
I had to go and put dad's broad beans in and the shallots. I was
11 or 12 or maybe 13 then. I used to knock them in as quick as
I could and then go off round the Old Road footballing.

The first time I went fishing, I've never forgot it, and I should
be about 8 or 9 then. There was an older boy name of Harris,
lived up our street, he was getting on for 14, and he said to me
when I was going to school in the afternoon, "Bill, I'm going
fishing, will you come?"

I said, "Yes, I'll come with you mate".

So we went off fishing down the river by the viaduct. I got
home when we'd finished fishing in the afternoon, somewhere
before teatime, and mother said to me when I went in, "Where
have you been this afternoon?"

I said, "To school"

She said, "You've not".

I said, "I have!"

She said, "You've not, I've waited outside till all the children
came out and I went in and asked the teacher and she said you
hadn't been to school".

So then she said, "Well, where have you been then?"

So then I had to tell her. She had come to meet me out of
school because she was going to take me to the Market to buy
me a pair of boots. William never came out so I never had my
new boots.

She said, "You can get undressed".

I can see myself sitting behind the door now, and dad came

in the back way and said, "Hello what's the matter with him?"

"He hasn't been to school this afternocn", she said, "so you've got to deal with him".

The cane was hanging up on a nail, he got that cane off and he gave me about three or four clips before I could get up the blinking stairs. I had to stop in bed then, no tea. That's the first fishing I had.

When I had more time, when we were working four days a week in the later years, I used to go fishing over where the pits are now at Cosgrove, in the river there, there was only one pit at that time. I used to go down there early morning as soon as it was light and I got very friendly with a farmer, named Markham, and I was pleased to help them in the hayfield, I used to go up to his house and all. The 2 or 3 shillings he paid me used to make a lot of difference in those days, it was a lot of money. I used to get mushrooms from down there and used to bring bags of watercress up from out of the river. I used to take it into the Club and let some of the people have it. One day I'd arranged to help Mr. Markham one Monday morning and they hadn't come down with the tackle and the horses, so I started to walk up to the house, that's up against Castlethorpe station, and I'd got a black overcoat over my shoulder, walking up across the field, because I didn't know whether I should stop up there or not. I saw a hare sitting down there and I stood and looked at it and I thought, "Well William, what have I got to do with you?"

So I got a bit nearer and chucked my coat over the top and dropped on it. They shout, "Auntie, auntie, auntie" when they're caught, and so of course I got him up and knocked him on the back of the head, and I thought, "Now what have I got to do with it?"

There was a rickyard about half way up, so I thought I'd better cover it under some hay. I met them coming down, they'd just come over the railway bridge the farmer and his men and horses and waggons. "Arthur," I said, "I think I've transgressed".

He said, "Why, what's the matter Bill?"

"I saw a hare laying in the form," I said, "and I couldn't resist the temptation, I fell on it".

He said, "Well, what have you done with it?"

"Well I put it in the hay in the rickyard". And he said, "Alright Bill, but don't tell these men what've you've done. When we've gone up at night-time, you come and fetch it".

When they'd gone I went and fetched this hare and I sold it for 3/6d, which was a lot of money then.

Weekends I used to go fishing a lot and I used to go with a man the name of Horne down at Cosgrove. We used to have to go down by the Iron Trunk, down to the broadwaters and have a punt tied at the bottom there, where the old river used to come round. I had to walk down there and there was no gum boots then so I used to get a bit of cork lino and make a sole and cover it with canvas and soak well with boiled oil and let it dry. That's what I used to have to keep the wet out of my shoes. One Friday night I got my son-in-law, who's a wheelwright at Old Stratford to make me a knife to clean the rushes out. There was a big wide open space in the river there, and on the other side were all these big lily pads. I knew there were some fish in there so I took this knife down and cleaned the river out at night, early evening, and before I came away I took some bait with me and baited it up.

I got down there before it was light the next morning and, blimey, talk about fish, I brought 75 pound of bream home! I had 4 bream, each weighed 4¾lbs each. I got on the bus and I took my son-in-law and his father one each and I gave all the others away all round here — that's the best catch of bream I ever had.

My son-in-law knew the farmer between Deanshanger and the next village and the farmer let him go fishing there. We used to go down there of a Sunday morning. My daughter used to come and bring the bacon and eggs and frying pan and water and we used to go fishing. It was lovely, the smell of bacon and eggs cooking out in the open. We had a boat on the Thames once, we took it out from Oxford and we used to get out in the morning, soon as it was light, in our pyjamas, fishing.

Chapter 5
WAR SERVICE

At the time of the Boer War there were no telephones, not as we know them today. We used to get waiting for the boaties to come along and ask them if they'd got any news of the Boer War. The boats on the canal were horse-drawn and it was from the boaties that we learned this and that, because they touched other towns.

The relief of Mafeking, I remember that, everybody was drunk on that day, all they could say was "the relief of Mafeking". We heard about it first, I think, from the boaties. The pubs were open, they all came out of the Works and had the red flags that the guards held up. Everybody was drunk then — I wasn't!

During the First World War we were in reserved occupation. But it came so tight that we'd got no work and 3 of us volunteered to go in 1918. Some had already volunteered but I was getting on a bit by then, I'd got 4 kids. Three of us finally went to the Flying Corps. We had to go to Oxford. Of course they wanted to fling us in the blinking infantry and we wouldn't have it. They said, "You'll have to go to Cowley Barracks and stay the night".

"Oh no, we damn well shan't"

"You'll have to!"

So we got the reserved occupation tickets out and showed them these — that's how we got out of that!

We went through the ordinary routines in London and went down to Blandford to get fitted out and we were posted then up to a base about 6 miles out of Nottingham in a new aerodrome. We went on to the base and somebody tapped the window and it was a chap who lived up our street, he'd joined up 2 weeks before. It was cricketing time because when we were at Blandford I know that we'd been vaccinated and I went and had a game of cricket.

We were up near Nottingham for about 6 months, perhaps a bit more, then we were transferred to Cranwell, that's a big station, all sorts of aircraft, little ones and big ones, the big ones were 2 engined ones then; they'd got balloons too. I played football there. The jobs that I had to do mostly were patching the fabric of the planes up, it was all Irish linen then, all coated over with a sort of cellophane stuff. We had jolly good times at Cranwell, but we came home first leave we had. There was a wait to get your train pass and we didn't get our passes in time to catch the proper train which met the connection to Wolverton. We had to go through to Bletchley but it was a lovely moonlight night I remember. My mate lived at Bradwell and I lived here and I said "Come on, we'll go through Bletchley Park I've never been but we'll find a way somewhere".

But any road I lost my way a bit and we came out this side of Denbigh Hall. I left my mate at the 'Talbot Inn' at Loughton, he walked round that way through Bradwell, I came straight up the Watling Street and it was just breaking day when I got to Two Mile Ash.

I went up and had a look at my allotments that my dad and my younger brother were doing while I was away.

I had a different type of leave later on. You could put in for 'potato' leave if you'd got an allotment and I'd got the gout in my knees and I could hardly walk. Any road I managed it, I got down here but I had to go to bed. I got rid of the gout a bit, had 5 or 6 days leave, and I went and got some of my blinking potatoes out and the blinking gout came on again. I got a doctor's certificate and a J.P. to sign it and sent it off but they sent a telegram back "If you don't return we will send an escort" so I had to go back.

We got shifted from there to a station, against Kings Lynn. I've never come across such a place never — like bloody monkeys! Food? It was terrible! You had all your spuds cooked in their jackets. It was oilcloth on the tables and I'd only been there 2 days and it was lunchtime. We went in there and I got up and made a hell of a racket about it.

I said, "Why can't we have some boiled potatoes, have it like somebody else can have it, have 'em all peeled and have something on the table, not oilcloth?"

It was a wonder I hadn't got court-martialled but any road they elected me to go and see somebody else and they said "What? If you don't like it like that and if you can arrange to detail some men to do it, you can have it your way"

"Well", I said to the other 2 or 3 with me, "we can agree to that".

"Well I'll leave it to you to pick your men"

After that we had a different going-on.

The two men I went with, one was Jack Bull and the other one was Billy Wise. I screwed them both down in their boxes, one died at Bradwell and the other died up the street in Western Road. I remember the first one was Bull down at Bradwell and the undertaker, he'd put the screws in at the top and he had a pump screwdriver and I picked it up and I pumped the screws in. He looked at me and I said, "I pump hundreds and thousands of screws in my job at the Works".

And the same up there in Western Road he did the same trick practically, he had a pump screwdriver and I pumped them all in. We had to lift Billy Wise out through the window, he was only a little chap.

Chapter 6
CLUBS & ENTERTAINMENT

Wolverton Working Men's Club was started in Church Street about 4 houses the Stratford side of the Co-op shop — you can tell that because after those 4 houses there's a smaller house. My father was on the first lot of committees and they used to have the meetings in the Science and Arts Institute — everybody had a meeting in the Science and Arts Institute — and they started from that house. When dad didn't want to go out he used to send me for a pint of Guinness, mother always had Guinness, and perhaps some for him. You always carried it in a jug in those days. I used to go there and I couldn't reach the knocker, I used to have to kick the door. They had a doorkeeper on, same as they do now. He used to open the door and I can remember the blooming smoke used to come out, with a lot of men in two rooms and two rooms upstairs. They only used to smoke twist and Cavendish — that was the black tobacco.

After some years they got a bit of money together and when Walter Thurstone was Secretary they built this Club on the front. Of course it's been modernised 2 or 3 times. Walter Thurstone wanted to buy the whole piece where houses stand now, he'd got a good idea he had, foresight. He wanted to buy that for tennis courts and bowling greens and quoit pitches, which was all a go at that time. Of course they hadn't enough money to do it, but they borrowed the money off Bass's brewery. I've been round Bass's twice when I was on the committee. I can remember once going with the Secretary up to London, we also went round Whitbread's bottling place, that was up the Gray's Inn Road, and then we went for a meeting at the Head Office in Clerkenwell Road. I can remember another occasion when I was on the Catering Committee going to Northampton. We used to have our spirits from a Northampton brewery and we were getting short, in the War period, and you couldn't get any. The Chairman and the Secretary and I had to make an appeal at the brewery for some more stuff. Whether it came or not, I don't know.

I've been a member there ever since I was 21, there's only one member older than me and I think he's left the town now. Mild was 2d and the bitter was 3d a pint and that was beer that was. There was a chap working the other side of the bench to me in work he said on Thursday afternoon, "Bill how much money have you got?"

I said, "I don't know, why?"

I put my hand in my pocket, I'd got 6½d.

He said, "I've got a tanner. What do you say we have a night out tonight?"

I said, "Alright, I'll go and put our name down for billiards for half past 7".

We went there, we had three half pints each, a packet of Woodbines each and played a game of billiards, and we went home with some money in our pockets. I've related that many, many times and they can't believe it. And it used to be beer then. The Bass's bitter used to be racked up for a month before it was sold.

We had some big 60 or 80 gallon barrels and the first time that I went down in the cellar, we had to empty a barrel of rum — it used to come in about 32 gallons. I sat over there on a box, we had to measure it out in copper gallon cans, just get it to the top then they'd take it and tip it in the big vat, 60 gallons it must have been, maybe more, and I came up from that cellar nearly drunk, with the fumes from that rum. We had to measure it because the railwaymen would have a gimlet, drill the hole in the barrel and run it out and block it up again.

All Guinness stout used to come from Dublin, and it always used to be delivered by dray from the station's Goods shed. If there was four barrels to come up there were 4 blokes come one at a time, they'd bring one barrel at a time and have a pint of beer as their perk.

You could play dominoes, skittles, billiards, whist, but no gambling was allowed. You had quoits, and when I was on the committee down there, we had the Club done up, because it was all gas then, and in 6 months' time the place wanted doing up again. I had an idea to have electric light in so I contacted the foreman who was on the Maintenance Electric Light in the Works and talked to him about it and he said "Alright Bill".

I said, "Will you help me?"

He said, "Yes".

So I went to his house many times and got an estimate out, for what we thought it wanted, and what engine we'd got to have to run it, fuel and so forth. I put it before the Committee and it was discussed for some months and months and eventually they agreed to it.

It was started on and the War came along. We estimated a 4½h.p. engine to charge the batteries up. There was another man on the Committee, name of Cliff Anderson, he was in the Drawing Office over the Electric Department and he said, "You don't want a 4½h.p., it's too big".

They decided to have a 2½h.p.

It got under way and they kept adding better lights and then the Steward who was told how to use this here thing, he had to go in the Army, so they had to train another man and he had to go in the Army. In the finish the Chairman took it over then, and he used to drink nothing else but gin, and of course he used to keep going out to this doings at night when he'd finished work, and they called him 'Ginny' and they called the engine 'Ginny' "Going to see Ginny again?"

Gin was only 2½d a half quarter then, Whisky was 3/6d a bottle. Different stuff to what you get today.

That club got too small; it got overcrowded. If you wanted a seat on Sunday morning you had to be down there at ten minutes to 12 to get a seat. Some of them broke away and they started the Top Club like we did. They had their money from Higgins' brewery. They knew what was wanted from down the Bottom Club and they got the proper place. Since then that's all been modernised. They called that the 'Rhubarb Arms' because there were 6 fields of allotments alongside and the majority of allotment holders used to call in there coming from the allotments.

The first extension to the Bottom Club was the Billiards room. The billiard tables used to be from East to West — there were three and if you were sitting on the seat when a bloke was playing you would have to mind out or he'd knock you in the face with his cue. Then they put a piece on which lengthened it about half as much again and then they shifted the tables round lengthways so it made more room.

When they built it they did away with the quoit ground. I used to play quoits: my dad he was a good quoit player. It's a game played with steel rings and a bed of clay about 3 feet square. There's a steel peg drove in and you've got to get your quoit near that peg and if you were playing somebody else he tried to lay it on the top of your quoit.

They used to have concerts every Saturday, one at the Top Club and one at the Bottom Club. My mother and father used to go to them both. I've been there, me and my father and his pal, the name of Alf Walters he lived at Stony Stratford, we used to have a bottle of whisky between us, 3/6d.

We used to have artists from all over the country, practically. The majority of them came from London and Birmingham and Manchester. We had a damn good chap from Swindon he was a good singer, a tenor, I can remember him well. Once the artists couldn't get here for some reason and at the Picture Palace they used to run artists between a film and as they finished we got them at the two Clubs.

They used to have a Dinner at the Club. You had to pay a shilling and they kept coming round filling your glasses up with beer and you could have as much as you liked — some of them had four plates of blinking meat. I heard one bloke say, "What you can't eat, put on my plate".

Meat was meat then, different to what it is today.

When the Bottom Club started there was a controversy in the Press about people going down there on Sunday mornings, changing books, (of course there was a library at each Club). I said "We don't interfere with Churches, why should Churches interfere with us?"

When Mafeking was relieved, practically every man was drunk. They all had free beer from the 'Engineer's' the 'North Western' and the 'Victoria Hotel'. The pubs used to open at 6 o'clock in the morning in those days, and the chaps who wanted could go in and have a rum and milk and then go into work losing a quarter of an hour. There was not a great lot of drunkenness at that time. I always remember when I was a boy and lived down the Little Streets, on a Friday night when the pubs turned out, it used to be 10 o'clock there always used to be a fight outside. I always remember one, a chap the name of Alf, he'd pick a fight with somebody and there was generally a scrap out there.

I've never used the pubs much, you don't get the interference like that in the Club. If a person doesn't behave himself he's outside. And you don't get Salvation Army people coming round selling 'War Cry' you just chat with your pals.

Whitsun was always a big time in Wolverton. About 3 weeks

before Whitsuntide in the workshop opposite where the Club is now the men who used to repair the coaches all had to go 'day work' the metals that the coaches used to run on used to be filled up and made into a bandstand and everything was tidied up ready for a Ball on Whit Monday and Tuesday nights.

The Whit Monday they used to have one of the Guards' bands come. Crowds used to meet them off the train and they used to play from the station up to the Science and Arts Institute and they used to have their lunch there. They used to parade from there round the town and then they went to the Park. There were crowds, hundreds and hundreds down there and there were Whitsuntide sports.

When I was a boy, about 17 or 18, we used to go to the Ball and stop till it was finished and when we came out it was just breaking daylight and we walked along the canal side to Cosgrove to Castlethorpe back to Haversham and home for breakfast.

The Ball was organised by the Dancing Club. The Guards' band used to play on the Monday, but they weren't so good for dancing. Our own Bucks Volunteer Band used to play at several dances at the Science and Arts and they kept time better than the Guards did. They used to dance the Quadrilles, the Lancers, Waltzes, Barn Dance and Waltz Cotillions. One end was fitted up with a bar for drinks, whisky, brandy or whatever and the other end was all lemonades and cups of tea and coffee and minerals and cakes. The children came, but they didn't stop so late, because it didn't finish till nearly 3 o'clock in the morning.

It was always a good holiday Whitsuntide was and many of the old people who can remember it talk about it now.

FINAL THOUGHTS

Wolverton is a community, it was always the same, it never changed. The only time I ever remember it changing was when they built our houses up Cambridge Street. It never varied in all those years till they started extending. The houses were built by the Railway, so was the Church and the Science and Arts Institute.

You go out of Wolverton, as I did when I was on the Union Executive for 14 years, and had to travel a lot and you met people and they said "Oh, you're a Cockney". So I said, "I'm not", and they asked where you came from, and you always found somebody who knew Wolverton. The apprentices when they came out of their time had to leave Wolverton at one period and of course they travelled all over the world.

They used to say Wolverton was "piano and herrings" — that's what they used to live on! Of course nearly everybody had a piano, I've got one, but we've never lived on herrings, but I like fish and have always lived well. My mother and father used to look after us, we used to have hams hanging up and a side of bacon as well. We always lived well, we always had plenty of puddings, 'spotted dick', beef steak and kidney puddings. I had to go and do the shopping. I always remember, it sticks in my mind ever since, "6lb of moist sugar for 10½d", I knew that by heart. 3d a pint of milk, 1/-d a score of eggs — you don't realise: my missus bought a pound of sausages recently — 34 pence!

As far as Stony Stratford is concerned they didn't seem to cotton on with Wolverton somehow in the later years. It was alright in the earlier years. Bradwell people and Wolverton people seem to get on better than with Stony Stratford. As an illustration Stony Stratford wouldn't help with the swimming pool and there was a hell of a lot of fuss over that. There's no aristocrats in Wolverton or Bradwell, though there was some in Stratford and it made a difference.

I don't think society's any more equal today, because there's more millionaires than there's ever been, and now they're moaning.

There's a law for the rich and a law for the poor, isn't there? When somebody up the top does something wrong, they get away with it, but a poor man he has to suffer, he has to go through with it. You can take Profumo, being kicked out of Parliament: well, if a Labour man did that he'd be hung, drawn and quartered .

When I die, I'm going to be burnt. I'm on this earth because I was put here. It wasn't like Adam and Eve: they took a rib out of Adam to make Eve — if you can believe that!